Baby's First Bible

ABC

Written and designed by Johna Robbins

This Book Belongs To

....

A is for

ADAM

Genesis 2:20 (The first man!)

B is for

BATHSHEBA

1 King 1:15

C is for

CALEB

Numbers 14:30

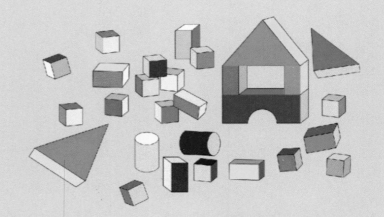

D is for

DANIEL

Daniel 6:21-22.

E is for

ELISABETH

Luke 1:41

F is for

FeLIX

Acts 23:24

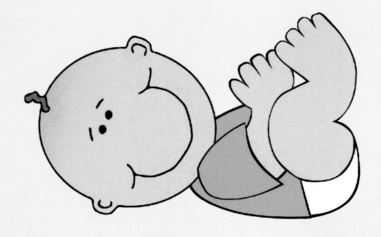

H is for

HABAKKUK

Habakkuk 1:1

G is for
GABRIEL
Luke 1:19

I is for

ISAIAH

2 Kings 19:6

J is for

JOSIAH

2 Kings 22:1

K is for

KING

1 Kings 1:4

L is for

LAZARUS

John 11:1

M is for

MARY

Matthew 1:18

N is for

NAOMI

Ruth 1:2

O is for

ORPAH

Ruth 1:4

P is for

PETER

Matthew 16:18

Q is for

QUARTUS

Roman 16:23

R is for

RACHEL

Genesis 29:10

S is for

SAMUEL

1 Samuel 1:20.

T is for

TAMAR

Genesis 38:6

U is for

URIAH

2 Samuel 11:8

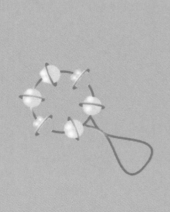

V is for

VASHTI

Esther 1:9 (Queen)

W is for

WATCHMAN

2 Samuel 18:24

x is for

xerxes

Esther 1:10 (AKA King Ahasuerus)

Y is for

YAHWEH

Exodus 3:14 (I AM THAT I AM)

Z is for

ZACHARIAH

2 Kings 15:8

THIS BOOK WAS MADE WITH

Created by: Johna Robbins

"KJV"

Made in the USA
Columbia, SC
11 June 2022